This Book is to be Read in Bed

Dr. Seuss'
SLEEP BOOK

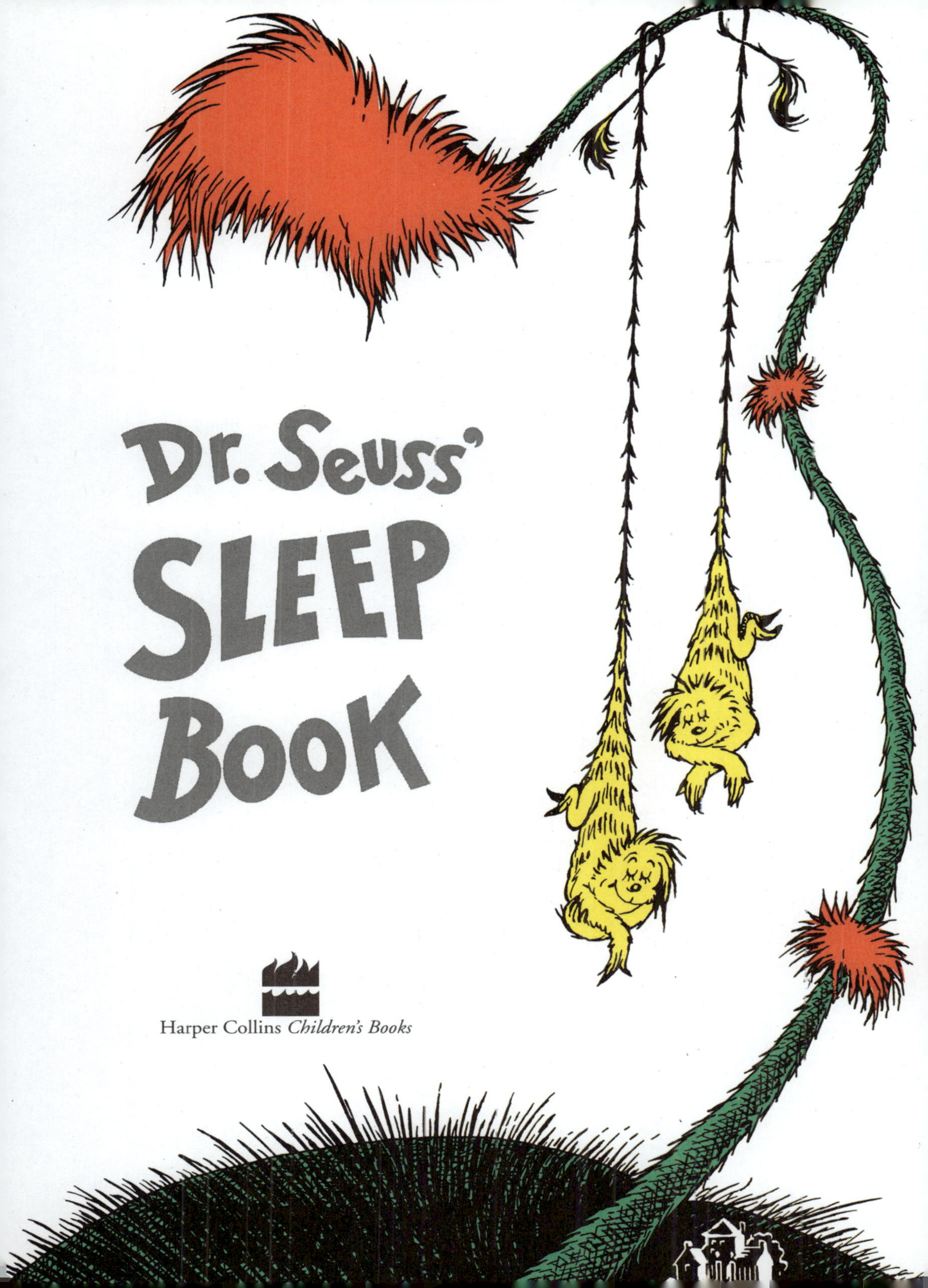

Harper Collins *Children's Books*

For Marie and Bert Hupp

1

ISBN 978 0 00 7414277

First published by Random House Inc.,
New York, USA
First published in the UK 1964
This edition published in the UK 2010 by
HarperCollins*Children's Books*,
a division of HarperCollins*Publishers* Ltd
77-85 Fulham Palace Road
London W6 8JB

Visit our website at:
www.harpercollinschildrensbooks.co.uk

Printed and Bound in India by
Gopsons Papers Ltd., Noida

The news
Just came in
From the County of Keck
That a very small bug
By the name of Van Vleck
Is yawning so wide
You can look down his neck.

This may not seem
Very important, I know.
But it *is.* So I'm bothering
Telling you so.

A yawn is quite catching, you see. Like a cough.
It just takes one yawn to start other yawns off.
NOW the news has come in that some friends of Van Vleck's
Are yawning so wide you can look down *their* necks.

At this moment, right now,
Under seven more noses,
Great yawns are in blossom.
They're blooming like roses.

The yawn of that one little bug is still spreading!
According to latest reports, it is heading
Across the wide fields, through the sleepy night air,
Across the whole country toward every-which-where.
And people are gradually starting to say,
"I feel rather drowsy. I've had quite a day."

Creatures are starting to think about rest.
Two Biffer-Baum Birds are now building their nest.
They do it each night. And quite often I wonder
How they do this big job without making a blunder.
But that is *their* problem.
Not yours. And not mine.
The point is: They're going to bed.
And that's fine.

Sleep thoughts
Are spreading
Throughout the whole land.
The time for night-brushing of teeth is at hand.
Up at Herk-Heimer Falls, where the great river rushes
And crashes down crags in great gargling gushes,
The Herk-Heimer Sisters are using their brushes.
Those falls are just grand for tooth-brushing beneath
If you happen to be up that way with your teeth.

The news just came in from the Castle of Krupp
That the lights are all out and the drawbridge is up.
And the old drawbridge draw-er just said with a yawn,
"My drawbridge is drawn and it's going to stay drawn
'Til the milkman delivers the milk, about dawn.
I'm going to bed now. So nobody better
Come round with a special delivery letter."

The number
Of sleepers
Is steadily growing.
Bed is where
More and more people are going.
In Culpepper Springs, in the Stilt-Walkers' Hall,
The stilt-walkers' stilts are all stacked on the wall.
The stilt-walker walkers have called it a day.
They're all tuckered out and they're snoozing away.
This is very big news. It's important to know.
And that's why I'm bothering telling you so.

Way out in the west, in the town of Mercedd,
The Hinkle-Horn Honking Club just went to bed.
Every horn has been quietly hung on a hook,
For the night, in its own private Hinkle-Horn Nook.

All this long, happy day, they've been honking about
And the Hinkle-Horn Honkers have honked themselves out.
But they'll wake up quite fresh in the morning. And then...
They'll all start Hinkle-Horn honking again.

Everywhere, creatures
Are falling asleep.
The Collapsible Frink
Just collapsed in a heap.
And, by adding the Frink
To the others before,
I am able to give you
The Who's-Asleep-Score:
Right now, forty thousand
Four hundred and four
Creatures are happily,
Deeply in slumber.
I think you'll agree
That's a whopping fine number.

Counting up sleepers . . ?
Just how do we do it . . ?
Really quite simple. There's nothing much to it.
We find out how many, we learn the amount
By an Audio-Telly-o-Tally-o Count.
On a mountain, halfway between Reno and Rome,
We have a machine in a plexiglass dome
Which listens and looks into everyone's home.
And whenever it sees a new sleeper go flop,
It jiggles and lets a new Biggel-Ball drop.
Our chap counts these balls as they plup in a cup.
And that's how we know who is down and who's up.

40, 404

Do you talk in your sleep . . ?
It's a wonderful sport
And I have some news of this sport to report.
The World-Champion Sleep-Talkers, Jo and Mo Redd-Zoff,
Have just gone to sleep and they're talking their heads off.
For fifty-five years, now, each chattering brother
Has babbled and gabbled all night to the other.

They've talked about laws and they've talked about gauze.
They've talked about paws and they've talked about flaws.
They've talked quite a lot about old Santa Claus.
And the reason I'm telling you this is because
You should take up this sport. It's just fine for the jaws.

Do you walk in your sleep . . ?
I just had a report
Of some interesting news of this popular sport.
Near Finnigan Fen, there's a sleepwalking group
Which not only walks, but it walks a-la-hoop!
Every night they go miles. Why, they walk to such length
They have to keep eating to keep up their strength.

So, every so often, one puts down his hoop,
Stops hooping and does some quick snooping for soup.
That's why they are known as the Hoop-Soup-Snoop Group.

Sleepwalking, too, are the Curious Crandalls
Who sleepwalk on hills with assorted-sized candles.
The Crandalls walk nightly in slumbering peace
In spite of slight burns from the hot dripping grease.
The Crandalls wear candles because they walk far
And, if they wake up,
Want to see where they are.

Now the news has arrived
From the Valley of Vail
That a Chippendale Mupp has just bitten his tail,
Which he does every night before shutting his eyes.
Such nipping sounds silly. But, reall , it's wise.

He has no alarm clock. So this is the way
He makes sure that he'll wake at the right time of day.
His tail is so long, he won't feel any pain
'Til the nip makes the trip and gets up to his brain.
In exactly eight hours, the Chippendale Mupp
Will, at last, feel the bite and yell "Ouch!" and wake up.

A Mr. and Mrs. J. Carmichael Krox
Have just gone to bed near the town of Fort Knox.
And they, by the way, have the finest of clocks.

I'm not at all sure that I quite quite understand
Just how the thing works, with that one extra hand.
But I *do* know this clock does one very slick trick.
It doesn't tick tock. How it goes, is tock tick.
So, with ticks in its tocker, and tocks in its ticker
It saves lots of time and the sleepers sleep quicker.

What a fine night for sleeping! From all that I hear,
It's the best night for sleeping in many a year.
They're even asleep in the Zwieback Motel!
And people don't usually sleep there too well.

The beds are like rocks and, as everyone knows,
The sheets are too short. They won't cover your toes.
SO, if people are actually sleeping in THERE...
It's a great night for sleeping! It must be the air.

It's a great night for snores! I just had a report
Of some boys who are tops in this musical sport.
The snortiest snorers in all our fair land
Are Snorter McPhail and his Snore-a-Snort Band.
This band can snore *Dixie* and old *Swanee River*
So loud it would make forty elephants shiver.

The loudest of all of the boys is McPhail.
HE snores with his head in a three-gallon pail.
So they snore in a cave twenty miles out of town.
If they snored closer in, they would snore the town down.

Do you know who's asleep
Out in Foona-Lagoona . . ?
Two very nice
Foona-Lagoona Baboona.

We've added them into our Who's-Asleep Count
Which has grown to a really amazing amount.
Exactly eight million, eight hundred and eight
Creatures are sleeping now! Isn't that great!

A Jedd is in bed,
And the bed of a Jedd
Is the softest
Of beds in the world,
It is said.
He makes it from pom poms
He grows on his head.
And he's sleeping right now
On the softest of fluff,
Completely exhausted
From growing the stuff.

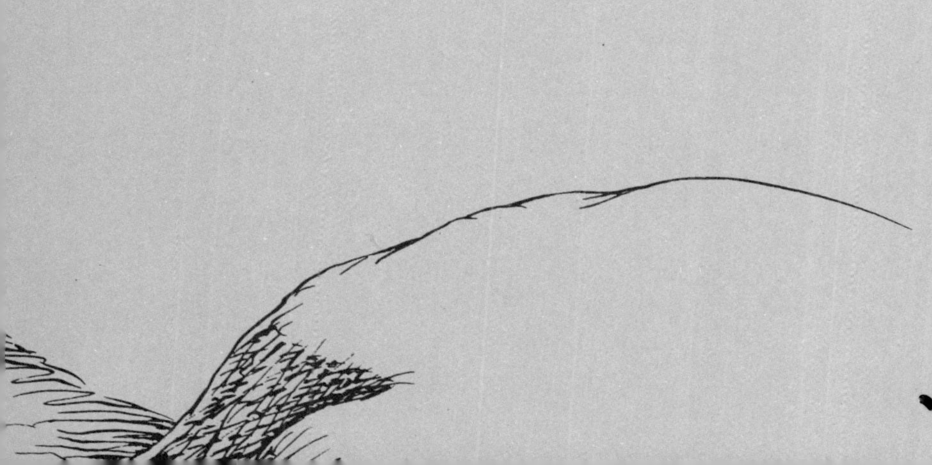

The news has come in from the District of Dofft
That two Offt are asleep and they're sleeping aloft.
And how are they able to sleep off the ground..?
I'll tell you. I weighed one last week and I found
That an Offt is SO light he weighs minus one pound!

THIS ONE, TOO,
PLEASE

A moose is asleep.
He is dreaming of moose drinks.
A goose is asleep.
He is dreaming of goose drinks.
That's well and good when a moose dreams of moose juice.
And nothing goes wrong when a goose dreams of goose juice.

But it isn't too good when a moose and a goose
Start dreaming they're drinking the other one's juice.
Moose juice, not goose juice, is juice for a moose
And goose juice, not moose juice, is juice for a goose.
So, when goose gets a mouthful of juices of moose's
And moose gets a mouthful of juices of goose's,
They always fall out of their beds screaming screams.
SO . . .
I'm warning you, now! Never drink in your dreams.

Speaking of dreaming,
I think you should note
That the Bumble-Tub Club Is now dreaming afloat.
Every night they go dreaming down Bumble-Tub Creek
Except for one night, every third or fourth week,
When they stop for repairs. 'Cause their bumble-tubs leak.
But tonight they're afloat, full of dreams, full of bliss,
And that's why I'm bothering telling you this.

At the fork of a road
In the Vale of Va-Vode
Five foot-weary salesmen have laid down their load.
All day they've raced round in the heat, at top speeds,
Unsuccessfully trying to sell Zizzer-Zoof Seeds
Which nobody wants because nobody needs.

Tomorrow will come. They'll go back to their chore.
They'll start on the road, Zizzer-Zoofing once more
But tonight they've forgotten their feet are so sore.
And that's what the wonderful night time is for.

Everywhere,
Creatures
Have shut off their voices.
They've all gone to bed
In the beds of their choices.

They're sleeping in nooks. And they're sleeping in cracks.
Some on their tummies, and some on their backs.
They're peacefully sleeping in comfortable holes.
Some, even, on soft-tufted barber shop poles.
The number of sleepers is now past the millions!
The number of sleepers is now in the billions!

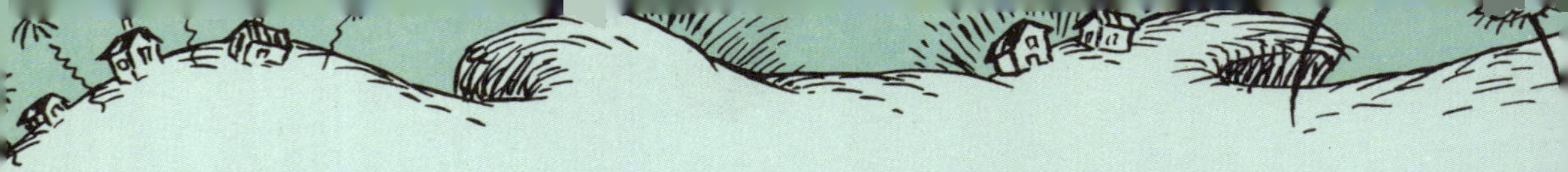

They're sleeping on steps! And on strings! And on floors!
In mailboxes, ships, and the keyholes of doors!
Every worm on a fishhook is safe for the night.
Every fish in the sea is too sleepy to bite.
Every whale in the ocean has turned off his spout.
Every light between here and Far Foodle is out.
And now, adding things up, we are way beyond billions!
Our Who's-Asleep-Score is now up in the Zillions!

Ninety-nine zillion,
Nine trillion and two
Creatures are sleeping!
So . . .
How about you?

When you put out *your* light,
Then the number will be
Ninety-nine zillion
Nine trillion and three.

Good night.

This Book is to be Read in Bed

Read them together, read them alone, read them aloud and make reading fun! With over 50 wacky stories to choose from, now it's easier than ever to find the right Dr. Seuss books for your child – just let the back cover colour guide you!

Here's a great selection to choose from:

Blue back books
for sharing with your child

Dr. Seuss's ABC
A Fly Went By
The Bears' Picnic
The Bike Lesson
The Eye Book
The Foot Book
Go, Dog, Go!
Hop on Pop
I'll Teach My Dog 100 Words
Inside Outside Upside Down
Mr. Brown Can Moo! Can You?
One Fish, Two Fish, Red Fish, Blue Fish
The Shape of Me and Other Stuff
There's a Wocket in my Pocket!

Green back books
for children just beginning to read on their own

A Fish Out of Water
And to Think That I Saw It on Mulberry Street
Are You My Mother?
The Bears' Holiday
Bears On Wheels
The Best Nest
The Cat in the Hat
The Cat in the Hat Comes Back
Come Over To My House
The Digging-est Dog
Fox in Socks
Gerald McBoing Boing
Green Eggs and Ham
Happy Birthday to YOU
Hunches in Bunches
I Can Read With My Eyes Shut!
I Wish That I Had Duck Feet
Marvin K. Mooney Will You Please Go Now!
Oh, Say Can You Say?
Oh, the Thinks You Can Think!
Ten Apples Up on Top
Wacky Wednesday

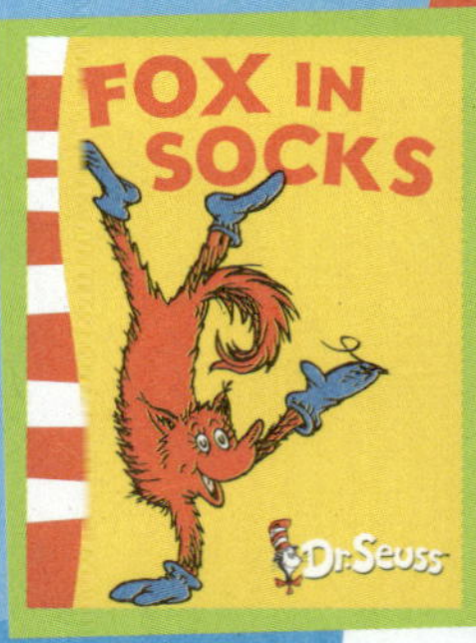

Yellow back books
for fluent readers to enjoy

The 500 Hats of Bartholomew Cubbins
Daisy-Head Mayzie
Did I Ever Tell You How Lucky You Are?
Dr. Seuss's Sleep Book
Horton Hatches the Egg
Horton Hears a Who!
How the Grinch Stole Christmas!
If I Ran the Circus
If I Ran the Zoo
I Had Trouble in Getting to Solla Sollew
The Lorax
McElligot's Pool
Oh, the Places You'll Go!
On Beyond Zebra
Scrambled Eggs Super!
The Sneetches and other stories
Thidwick the Big-Hearted Moose
Yertle the Turtle and other stories

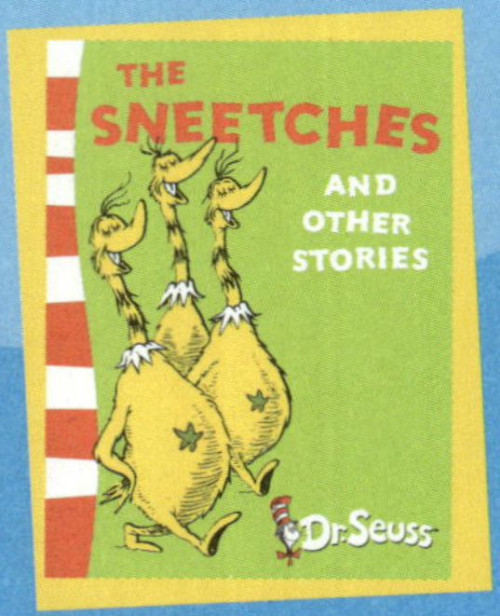